Andre's Dream

I Talk You Talk Press

CONTENTS

1. YOU MUST BUY A HOUSE

Andre wants to get married. He has a girlfriend. Her name is Sofia.

She says, "I want to get married too. But first, you have to buy a house. I don't want to get married until we have a house to live in."

Andre is surprised. "But I love you. If you love me, we can get married. We can rent an apartment. Then, we can save money and buy a house together," he says.

Sofia has blonde hair and blue eyes. She is very pretty. She works in a cosmetics shop. She lives with her parents, so she can spend all her money on clothes. Also, she is lucky because she gets cosmetics from work very cheaply. Sometimes they are free. Sofia always looks beautiful. Andre is very happy that she is his girlfriend.

"No, Andre. If I will be a married woman, I want a house."

"But Sofia. I don't have much money. I can't buy a house!"

Sofia holds Andre's hands. She looks into his eyes. "Of course you can. You are my hero. You can do anything!"

Andre laughs. But he is worried. He has saved a little money but it is not enough to buy a house. He works hard at the factory, but he spends most of his money taking Sofia out. She likes to go to the movies and to restaurants. She likes to ride in big cars. Andre doesn't have a car, but sometimes he hires a big car and drives Sofia and her friends around the city. Also, Sofia likes presents. She likes Andre to buy her things.

Andre goes to see an estate agent. The agent buys and sells houses. His name is Kovac. He shows Andre pictures of many, many houses.

"I cannot buy any of these houses," he tells the agent. "They are too expensive."

"Houses are expensive," says the agent. "Many people from other countries in Europe want to buy houses in Slovakia now. They think our houses are cheap. I cannot help you."

Andre looks very unhappy, so the agent asks him, "You are only a young man. Why do you want to buy a house?"

"I want to get married. My girlfriend says she won't get married until we have a house."

The agent thinks, *This young man should get another girlfriend.* But he doesn't say that. He says, "There is another house. It is very old. There is a toilet but it has no bathroom. It has been empty for fifty years. I will send an email to the owner. Maybe he wants to sell it. I will call you when I have an answer to my email."

Two days later the agent calls Andre. "The owner wants to sell it. It is very cheap. I think the condition of the house is very bad. But if you want to look at it, I will take you."

The agent drives Andre to the edge of the city. The house is near a road. There are fields all around the house. There is a stone fence, but there is no gate. The garden is full of rubbish. It is autumn, so there are no leaves on the trees around the house. It looks very grey and lonely. Andre and the agent go inside. The house is old and dark and very dirty. There are six rooms downstairs and two rooms upstairs. There is furniture in most of the rooms. It is very dusty. There are holes in the seats of the chairs and in the curtains.

"There are rats," says the agent. "I'm sorry. I have not been to see this house for a long time. The condition is worse than before. You will not want to buy this house."

"But I like it," says Andre. "I think I could make this into a beautiful home. There is electricity. The toilet works. There is water in the kitchen. The stove is very old but I think it will work. Later I will buy a new stove."

"But there is no bathroom!" says the agent.

"Maybe that's OK," says Andre. "I work in a factory. We make baths, basins and toilets. I think I can get everything I need for a good price."

The agent is not sure. But Andre is very sure. He wants to buy the house.

The agent and Andre go back to the agent's office. The estate agent tells Andre the price. It is very cheap, but it is still too expensive for Andre.

"The bank will not lend you any money," says the agent. "Not for this house. They want people to buy new houses."

Andre is very unhappy. "Thank you for showing me the house. You have been kind. But I understand it is impossible."

Andre goes back to his apartment. He collects his mail from the mailbox. There is a letter in a large white envelope. It is from a lawyer in Kosice. Andre opens the letter. His Great Uncle Gregor has died. He has left Andre some money. It is not a lot but …

Andre gets a pencil and paper. He calculates everything. With Uncle Gregor's money and his savings – maybe he can buy the house! He will live in it. He will save the rent from his apartment. He will have a little money to spend on fixing the house.

Andre calls the agent. "I think I can buy the house! I will come to see you tomorrow."

2. I HAVE BOUGHT A HOUSE!

A month later, all the paperwork is finished. Andre doesn't tell Sofia. He wants it to be a surprise. When Andre finishes work on Friday, he goes with the agent to a property lawyer's office. He signs all the papers and pays the money. Everything in the house is included.

"I think everything in the house is junk," says the lawyer. "You will have to throw it all away."

"I don't know," answers Andre. "I don't own any furniture, so I can use some of it until I get something better."

The lawyer hands Andre the owner's papers to the house.

"Congratulations," he says.

"Thank you," answers Andre. He looks at the owner's papers.

It says,

---*The house belonged to a family called Kovac.*---

Andre looks at the house agent. "Your name is Kovac, too."

The house agent and the lawyer smile. "You know that Kovac is a very common name. But yes, you are right," says the agent. "The house belonged to my family. To my brother and me. Before I showed you this house, I asked my brother, 'Can we sell it?' He said, 'OK'."

"But now, Andre," says the lawyer. "It belongs to you!"

Andre is very excited. He calls Sofia. "I have a surprise for you!"

"Oh, good! I love surprises," says Sofia.

"I will come and collect you after work tomorrow. What time will you finish?"

"The shop is open until eight o' clock, but I can leave at four."

"I will meet you outside the shop at four then."

Andre hires a car. He doesn't really have enough money, but it is a special occasion.

Andre meets Sofia at 4:00pm on Saturday. She looks very beautiful.

"What's the surprise?" she asks. "Have you bought me a present?"

"Wait and see," says Andre.

Andre drives Sofia to the house. "Look Sofia! I have bought a house! We can get married! It looks old and dirty now, but I will make it beautiful for you!"

Sofia looks out of the car window. "Are you crazy? I want a proper house! In the city! I want everything new and expensive. This looks like something for farm animals!"

Sofia will not get out of the car. She is very angry.

"You are so stupid Andre! You don't understand anything. Take me back into the city. I wore my best dress because you said you had a surprise for me. Take me to the Grand Hotel for dinner."

"I can't do that Sofia. I spent all my money on this house. I want to make a home for us. I have no money to take you out on a date."

"Well take me back into the city. I will call my girlfriends and go out with them."

Andre takes Sofia back into the city.

He takes the car back to the rental company. He collects his bicycle and cycles back to his apartment.

He cannot understand it. He loves Sofia. Sofia said she loved him. Andre bought a house for her. One day the house will be very beautiful. But Sofia doesn't want a house like this.

He sits in the dark in his apartment. He feels very upset. Finally he falls asleep.

The next morning, Andre is cold and hungry. He is also very sad. He takes his pencil and paper and looks at the numbers again. He cannot live in his apartment. He doesn't have enough money. He has to leave the apartment and go to live in his house. He calls his friend from the factory. His friend's name is Petr. Petr wants to find an apartment. Petr lives with his uncle and aunt but they have many children and they want Petr to move out.

"If you want my apartment, you can come and live here from today," Andre tells Petr. "Next week we can talk to the owner of my apartment. We can change the paperwork from me to you. But you can come today."

Petr has a small truck. Late in the day, he comes with all his belongings. Andre has packed all his things in boxes and bags. It is not very much. Clothes and books, some pots and pans, and an old television.

"I wish I had a television," says Petr.

"You can buy this one," says Andre. "I don't want it."

Petr gives Andre some money for the television. He also gives Andre some money for the rent for the rest of the month. Andre helps Petr bring everything from the little truck up to the apartment. Then Andre and Petr carry Andre's bags and boxes down to the truck. They put Andre's bicycle on top. Then they drive to Andre's new house. Petr is shocked when he sees the house. He likes Andre very much, so he doesn't say bad things about the house. He says, "It's a big house! It has a big garden too! When you have finished working on it, it will be great! I will come and help you."

It is dark now. Petr drives away. Andre walks into his house. He has brought a big sheet of plastic and some newspapers with him. He puts the plastic on the floor in the living room. Then he puts the newspapers on top. He takes some blankets from one of his boxes and makes a bed. He eats some bread and cheese and drinks some bottled water. He lies down in the dark. *I hope the rats stay away,* he thinks and he falls asleep.

3. A LONG COLD AUTUMN AND WINTER

The next morning it is raining. It rains all week. Andre has to cycle for thirty minutes to get to work. He is cold and wet and tired every day.

All week he is very unhappy. He tries calling Sofia but she won't talk to him. He fixes the old stove in the kitchen so he can make coffee and heat up soup. He fixes the lights in the living room so he doesn't have to live in the dark. He cleans the wooden table. He finds an old wooden chair and cleans that too. But he doesn't do anything else. Every night he sits at the table and thinks, *I'm so stupid! Why did I buy this house?*

On Saturday, it stops raining. The sun is shining. Andre feels better.

He thinks, *I will show Sofia! I will make this a beautiful house. She will see it and she will love it. I was stupid to show it to her before I fixed it.*

Andre takes the old curtains out into the garden behind the house. He takes out the old carpets and mattresses and pillows. He makes a fire and burns everything. Then he starts to take out all the furniture. He thinks he will burn that too. But then he stops and looks at it. Some of the furniture is very old but it looks good. Andre thinks he can use it. Andre takes everything out of one of the rooms downstairs. He cleans the room very well.

I will keep some of the furniture. I will keep it in this room. When I have time, I will clean and polish it. It's very good furniture, he thinks.

Andre has no money to go out with his friends. He has no money to go drinking or to go to football matches. When he gets paid, he spends the money on things for his house. All autumn and winter, Andre works on the inside of the house. The house still looks very bad outside. But the weather is too cold and wet and snowy to work in the garden.

By spring, the inside of the house looks very different. Andre has fixed the kitchen and the living room and one bedroom upstairs. The windows are clean and the floors are polished. The walls and ceilings are painted.

The factory has a big order for the Grand Hotel. They are making new modern bathrooms. The hotel is throwing all the old baths, basins and toilets away.

Andre asks the builder at the hotel, "Can I have some old baths, basins and toilets?"

The builder says "yes".

Petr and Andre take Petr's truck to get a bath, a basin and a toilet. There are many to choose from.

"Take two of everything!" says Petr. "You can make a big bathroom upstairs and another small bathroom downstairs."

Andre also takes taps and shower units.

Andre finishes the bathrooms. They look very good. The basins and baths are a little old fashioned but they suit the house.

They look better than modern ones, thinks Andre. *The kitchen looks good too.*

Petr's aunt wants a new kitchen. Petr says to his aunt, "Andre and I will help. We will take your old kitchen away. If we take the old kitchen out before the builder comes, it will save money."

Petr's aunt says, "OK."

Andre and Petr take the cupboards and counter from the kitchen. They are made of dark wood. Petr's aunt doesn't like them, but Andre likes them very much.

"They will look good in my old house," he says.

Andre has carefully cleaned and polished the old furniture. Some of it is very beautiful. There are no curtains. "I will not put curtains in the house," Andre tells Petr. "Sofia will want to choose the colours and patterns for the curtains."

Petr is worried. He thinks it is very sad that Andre thinks Sofia will come back to him. Petr has seen Sofia with another man many times in the town. The man has a big car. He looks rich.

Even if the house is wonderful, Sofia will never be Andre's girlfriend again, thinks Petr.

4. MAKING A GARDEN

When spring comes, Andre stops working on the inside of the house.

It's a good time to start working in the garden, he thinks. *I will work in the garden for a few weeks then I will fix the other rooms in the house.*

Andre starts working in the garden. There is a lot of rubbish. The house was empty for a long time. Some people from the city came here and threw their rubbish into the garden.

Andre makes many fires behind the house. Some things he can't burn. Petr comes in his truck and takes the rest of the rubbish to the city rubbish dump.

When all the rubbish is gone, Andre looks at the garden. It is a mess. There are some beautiful big trees along the sides of the garden. But there is nothing else.

Maybe I can buy some plants, thinks Andre.

Andre knows nothing about gardening. He goes to a second-hand bookshop in the city. He buys a book about gardening.

He starts working. He has no money to buy plants, but he can tidy the garden. The days are longer, so Andre can spend some time in the garden when he comes home from work.

One Saturday, Andre is working in the garden when he sees a man walk past the house. This is surprising. There are no houses nearby. Cars pass the house but no one walks so far from the city.

Andre smiles and waves to the man. "Nice day," he says.

The man smiles and waves back. The man stops and looks at the house. Then he walks away.

After that, Andre often sees the same man. He is about sixty years old. He walks along the road. He stops and looks at the house. Then he turns and walks away. Andre thinks it is very strange.

About two weeks later, Andre decides to cut down a tree. The tree is very old. It has no leaves. Andre thinks it will not live. When the tree is on the ground, Andre tries to carry it to the back of the house. He wants to burn it but the tree is very heavy. It is too heavy for him to carry. He sees the man again. The man stops and comes into the garden. He says something to Andre but Andre does not understand. The man moves his arms.

Then, Andre understands. The man will help him. "Thank you!" he says.

It is very difficult to carry the tree. Finally they are successful.

They are hot. It was hard work. Andre goes into the house. He brings water for the man and for himself.

"Thank you," says the man.

"Thank you," says Andre. The man goes away.

After that, the man comes every time Andre is working outside. He always helps Andre. Sometimes he speaks, but Andre cannot understand him. The man speaks English. The man knows a few words of Andre's language. He knows *hello, goodbye, thank you, please, stop* and a few other words.

Andre knows a few words in English. He tries to speak to the man. He asks the man his name.

"I am David Smith," says the man.

Each time, when they have finished working, David comes into the house. He walks around. He looks at everything. Sometimes he touches the furniture.

"Beautiful," he says.

Andre knows this word in English but he cannot have a conversation. The man does not speak Andre's language. It is very difficult. Andre can read English a little, but he cannot understand spoken English. Andre wants to tell David about his plans for the house and the garden. He wants to thank him for all the help.

Andre goes to the Internet café in the city. He finds some translation software. He finds out how to say, Could you please help me to learn English? I want to talk to you properly. Petr tries to help Andre to practice these words. But it is no good. Petr is not good at English.

So Andre prints the words on the printer in the Internet café. The next time David comes to the house, Andre gives him the paper. David reads it. He smiles.

"Yes, I will," he says. After that, when David comes, they speak in English. David gives Andre lists of words. Andre says the words many times.

David says, "Ten new words a day."

Andre practices ten words a day.

David also says, "Use it or lose it." Andre does not understand. "When your English is better, you will understand," says David.

Slowly the garden improves, and Andre's English improves. He asks David, "Where do you live?" But David doesn't answer. He asks David, "Why did you come to Slovakia?" But David doesn't answer. He asks David, "Why are you helping me?" David laughs and says, "I like gardening!"

David sometimes brings plants. They don't come from a plant shop. They come from a garden. They are wrapped in newspaper.

Andre has not seen Sofia for a long time. He heard that she has a new boyfriend. Andre thinks, *I don't mind. It doesn't matter. Isn't that strange? I am so busy and I have a new friend, and I am learning English. Life is very interesting. I am happy.*

It is almost summer. David has been coming to help Andre after work and on the weekends for almost three months. One day he says, "I must go away. But I will come back to see you."

Andre is very sad. He doesn't know anything about David. But Andre knows that David is his friend. He wants him to come back soon.

Most of the work in the garden is finished. Andre can start working on the inside of the house again. But he feels lonely. He is happy because he can speak some English, but he is worried. He understands the meaning of 'use it or lose it' now. *If I don't use English, I will forget it,* he thinks.

Petr has an idea. "There is an English school near our factory. Why don't you go?"

"I can't. I have no money and I must work on the house."

"The class is very cheap. And you need to have some free time. You never go out. Go!" says Petr.

5. ENGLISH CLASSES

Andre goes to the English school.

"We have beginner classes and intermediate classes," says the woman in the office.

Andre wants to join the beginner class. The first class is on Thursday evening. Andre is very nervous. He arrives early. He sits in the classroom. Other people arrive. There are about twelve people in the class. There are some businessmen and some students. There are two women who look like housewives.

I shouldn't be here! thinks Andre. *These people have a lot of education. I'm a factory worker. This is not for me.*

Andre stands up to leave, but the teacher comes in.

The teacher wants them to listen to English and to speak English. She asks everyone to introduce themselves. Andre listens to other people. When it is his turn, he is very shy.

"Good evening everyone," he says. "I am Andre. I work in a factory. My hobbies are gardening and fixing my house. I like watching football too, but my house and garden take all my money and my time. I am studying English so I can talk to my friend."

When Andre sits down everyone claps. The teacher says, "That was very good, Andre. Your English is good."

Andre enjoys the class. The teacher wants the students to talk a lot. Andre knows many words. He can understand the teacher's English.

After the class one of the younger people talks to him. "Your English is great! How long have you been studying?"

"About three months," says Andre.

"Only three months! I'm amazed! But you studied English in school, right?"

"I was a bad student in my schooldays. I never studied. I left school when I was fifteen. I learnt a few words of English but not very much."

"I'm Jakub. I have been studying English hard for more than ten years. I'm a university student. It's our vacation now. I learn about English literature at my university but we never speak in English. So I joined this conversation class. My listening and speaking ability is weak."

Andre says, "I can't read or write English very much. But I got a lot of practice speaking and listening."

"You're lucky! Did you go to England?"

"No I have an English-speaking friend. So I can speak English a little."

"Wow!"

After the next class Jakub says, "Maybe we can meet sometimes. We can practice speaking English together."

"I don't have a lot of free time," says Andre. "I'm fixing an old house. When I'm not at the factory I work in the house and the garden."

"I'll come and work with you!" says Jakub. "We can talk while we are working."

"I'm sorry, Jakub. I have no money. I can't pay you."

"No, no! My parents have a lot of money. I don't need a job. I just want to speak English more."

Jakub comes to help Andre on Saturdays and Sundays. Jakub works hard. They practice speaking English. Andre likes Jakub, but he misses David very much.

Jakub and Andre are fixing more of the rooms.

"The house is great, and I like the furniture. But why are there no curtains?" asks Jakub.

Andre doesn't want to talk about Sofia. He wanted to live in the house with Sofia. He wanted Sofia to choose the curtains. But he doesn't want to tell Jakub about that.

"I'll get curtains sometime," says Andre. "But they are expensive."

Usually Jakub rides his motor bike when he comes to help Andre. But the next day, he arrives in a car. It is an old car but it is very big.

"This is my father's old car," he says. "He gave it to me. But I like my motor bike more. I drove the car today because I have something for you. Come and help me."

Andre goes to the car. On the back seat are many curtains.

"My grandmother died in January. We moved into her old house. But my mother didn't like the curtains, so she bought new ones for every room. These curtains are old but the condition is good. There are more in the boot of the car."

The curtains are wonderful. The colours are dark – red, blue, green. Some of the curtains have gold thread and fringes. Andre likes them very much.

"Thank you Jakub! I must give your mother some money. These are very good quality."

"No, don't do that. She told my father and me to burn them."

It takes a long time to hang the curtains, but two weeks later, all the windows in the house have curtains. The house is looking very good.

Soon it is time for Jakub to go back to university.

He says to Andre, "I had a great vacation. I enjoyed talking with you. I liked working on this house and garden. I will come and see you the next time I'm at home. Oh, and I want to give you my car. I can't take it to university. I have no parking space at university and I like my motor bike. If you have enough money to pay the insurance, you can have it. My father will come and see you. He will bring the papers."

"I can't take your car!" Andre is embarrassed.

"Well it is really my father's car. He is very pleased with you. He wants you to have the car."

"I never met your father!"

Jakub laughs. "No, but this vacation I have worked every day. I have studied English. My English is better. I have worked with you in the house and the garden. My father is rich, but once he was very poor. He believes in hard work. My father usually says I am lazy, but this vacation he thinks I am a better man. Take the car!"

6. TWO BROTHERS

At the end of the summer, Mr Kovac, the estate agent, calls Andre.

"I would like to come and visit you," he says. "I would like to see the old house."

"Of course, Mr Kovac," says Andre. "You can come anytime."

"I'll come on Saturday afternoon," replies Mr Kovac. "Will that be OK?"

"Yes, that will be fine. See you then."

On Saturday afternoon, Mr Kovac arrives. Andre cannot believe it. Sitting in the car is David Smith!

Andre is very happy. Mr Kovac and David get out of the car.

"I believe you know this gentleman?" says Mr Kovac smiling.

"Yes, yes!" Andre shakes hands with the two men. "Come in, come in!"

They go inside. It is hot, so Andre has soda and beer on the table.

"You've done a great job!" says Mr Kovac. "I remember this house last autumn! It was in a very bad condition!"

Andre does not answer. He is staring at Mr Kovac. "You are speaking English!" he says.

"Of course," answers Mr Kovac. "My brother only speaks English. I had to learn English so I could talk to him!"

"But you look different!" says Andre.

"Well yes," says David. "Josef is tall and thin and I am short and fat. But we are brothers."

"You have different names!"

"Please don't call me Mr Kovac. You call my little brother David.

16

So you can call me Josef. Shall we sit down and have some beer? We will explain."

They sit down in the living room. The room is very clean. The furniture is shining. The curtains look great. Andre pours beer for everyone.

"David, please explain," he says.

"Josef and I were born in this house. He is six years older than me. He was born in 1950 and I was born in 1956. Life here was very difficult after the war. Our mother's aunt lived in England. She invited our family to join her. Our mother wanted to go very much. Our father did not. He did not want to leave his mother alone. They argued about it a lot. Finally, our mother took me and went to England. I was two years old. Josef stayed here with our father."

"Our father was very sad," says Josef. "He loved our mother very much. He loved David very much. He didn't want to live in this house without our mother. So he and I went to live with his mother, our grandmother. He hoped we could go to England later. But later it was impossible to leave Slovakia."

"Our mother took me to England. She changed our name to Smith. She wrote my name, David, in the English way. She wanted to forget everything about her life here. She never spoke Slovak. I guess I knew a few words when we went to England. But I was only two. I forgot the words. I didn't know anything about life in Slovakia," says David.

"When our father died, he left this house to David and me. I remembered David well. I was eight when he went to England," says Josef. "I wanted to find my brother. It was difficult, and it took a long time. My friend, the lawyer, helped me. Finally we found David Smith. I wrote to him and I went to England to meet him."

"It was terrible!" laughs David. "Josef spoke only a few words of English and I didn't speak Slovak. We were brothers but we hadn't seen each other for more than forty years and we didn't have a common language."

"I promised David I would learn English. I thought it would be good for business. I have been to England five times now. I studied very hard. My English is not great but it is good enough," says Josef.

David looks at Andre. "You went to see Josef. You wanted to buy a house, but you didn't have enough money for a normal house. But Josef likes you. So Josef sent me an email. He said, 'Why don't we sell the house? I will never live in it. I have my own house. You will never live in it. You live in England. Let's sell the house to this young man. Then you can take a long vacation, and come to Slovakia. You can spend the money from selling the house. Come back to Slovakia and learn about your birthplace!' He is my big brother. I always listen to him. So I agreed," says David.

Andre goes to the kitchen and brings back more beer. This is a long story!

"I am a teacher," explains David. "I asked my school for a long vacation. They agreed. So I came here."

"Are you an English teacher?" asks Andre.

"No. I teach maths."

"David came and stayed with me and my family. Of course, David wanted to see this house because he was born here. He said 'If I go to the house, maybe I will remember something'," says Josef

"Could you remember anything?" asks Andre.

"No. Nothing. I was too young. But I wanted Josef to come and look. He was older when he left this house. I think that he can remember a little."

"Yes," says Josef. "Later I would like to walk around the house. I remember some things."

"But why did you help me in the garden?" asks Andre.

Josef laughs. "David came and stayed with me and my family. But we are busy every day, even Saturdays and Sundays. So in the daytime he was bored."

"Gardening is my hobby. I love making new gardens. This garden was special to me. I can't remember anything, but when I was very young, I played in this garden."

"David took many plants from the garden of my house to give to you. My wife was very angry!" says Josef. "But I said, 'let him do it. The plants are for the garden of our childhood home'."

"And now, you are back," says Andre. "Do you plan to stay?"

"No. My life is in England. I have come for the wedding of Josef's daughter. I'm only staying for a week."

"I'd like you to stay longer," says Andre. "You taught me English. You are a great teacher and you are my friend. When will I see you again?"

"Wait and see", says David, smiling. "I thought 'I will never see my brother again'. But I did see him. Life is surprising. Wait and see."

7. A SURPRISE

Andre still goes to English classes. He didn't stay in the beginner's class very long. The teacher said, "You should be in the intermediate class. You are not a beginner."

Andre feels very proud. *I was a lazy student at school and I left school when I was fifteen years old. But I can learn a language!*

The house is very comfortable now. There are some more rooms to fix but Andre is not hurrying. *I have a living room, a kitchen, a dining room, two bathrooms and a bedroom!* he thinks. *That is enough for one person. I will take a break.*

Andre has more free time. Sometimes he and Petr meet after work and go to a bar. They always eat lunch together. But Andre likes to stay home. He doesn't go out with other friends. He doesn't go to football matches.

He listens to music and he reads English books. He doesn't have a computer but he can go to Josef's office on Saturdays and use the computer there. He doesn't drive his car very much, but he drives to work when it is raining.

I am a very boring person, thinks Andre. *But I don't care. I like my life. I am happy.* This is true, but one thing would make him happier. He would like to travel. He would like to go to England to see David and to study English, but Andre cannot go because he does not have enough money. *If I don't spend any money fixing the house, maybe in two years I can save enough money to go,* he thinks.

David said to Andre 'life is surprising'. Andre did not believe him. Then in one week, Andre gets two surprises.

Josef calls Andre on Saturday. "Can you come to the office now? I want to talk to you about something."

"Of course," says Andre. Andre is surprised. He hasn't seen Josef for a few weeks. Andre goes to Josef's office. Josef is excited.

"I have something to tell you! Sit down! About twenty years ago, I bought an old castle. The owner was an old lady. But she lived in Bratislava. The old lady was very poor. No one wanted to buy the castle. She wrote to me and asked me to help her. I couldn't find anyone to buy it either. So I bought it myself. I never told anyone about it. Not even my wife.

"Now I have found a buyer. It is a property company in England! They want to buy the old castle and turn it into a hotel. They are going to build small cottages in the grounds for more guests, tennis courts, a golf course, everything! I got a good price. But I am closing this office. I am not going to sell houses any more. The company came to me and asked me to work for them. I will manage everything here. They want me to work for them because I speak English and I know the city very well."

"That's great," says Andre.

"Yes!" says Josef. "I said 'Yes, I will take the job, but I need my assistant to come and work for me'."

Andre looks around the office. It is small. Sometimes Josef's wife is there. She does the paperwork. But she never goes to the office on Saturdays.

"Josef," says Andre. "You don't have an assistant."

"I do now," shouts Josef. "You!"

"Me?" Andre thinks Josef is crazy.

"There is so much work to do. The company managers will come here in November to look at everything. I will need help. These people are English. I need an English-speaking assistant!"

"But Josef. You can hire someone from a university. You can hire a great English speaker!"

"Yes, I can. But I won't know them! I know you like my own son. I know you can work hard. I know you are honest. I will hire expensive translators and lawyers and engineers with perfect English. But I want an assistant like you. Please say yes."

Andre thinks about the idea.

"Josef? Are you sure this company is real? If I leave my job at the factory and the company changes its mind about the hotel, I will have no job."

"I thought about that too," says Josef. "I said to the company, 'I want a job and money for three years. Even if there are problems and the project stops, you have to pay me and my assistant for three years.' The company said OK. Three years is a long time. If the project is a success, there will be other projects and more work for us. The company will pay you much more than the factory pays you. Please say yes!"

Andre thinks some more. Last year he spent all his money on buying a house. Why did he do that? Because he knew the house was right for him. He thinks about Josef and the new job. Does it feel right? Yes it does.

Andre jumps up and hugs Josef. "Yes, OK!"

"Andre, please do not tell anyone about this job. Not yet. In November, when the company managers come, they want to make a big announcement. Until then, it is a secret. But I want you to leave your job now. They will start paying us from next month. You can take a vacation first. After we start working on this project there will be no time for vacations."

"OK," says Andre. "I can finish the work on my house."

"No!" Josef shouts. "You are going to England. You are going to stay with David for three weeks. I want you to practice English very hard."

"That would be wonderful," says Andre. "But…"

Andre doesn't have enough money to go to England. But he doesn't want to tell Josef.

"I will pay for your air ticket," says Josef. "When the company starts to pay you, you can pay me back. Do you agree?"

Andre smiles at Josef.

"Yes. Of course! I really want to go to England. I want to improve my English. Thank you!"

8. SOFIA COMES BACK

David told Andre that life is surprising. Andre has a new job and a new future. He is going to England. But his life has one more surprise for him: Sofia.

Sofia is in a bar in the city. She is with her girlfriends. Her boyfriend broke up with her. She has no boyfriend. Sofia doesn't like this. She wants someone to take her out and buy her presents. She wants a new boyfriend.

Sofia looks around the bar. *Are there any rich men here?* she thinks. She sees Petr and his friends. They have been to a football match. They are drinking a lot and talking loudly. Sofia listens. They are talking about Andre! Sofia cannot hear everything but she hears Petr say, "Andre is going to England for a vacation!"

Sofia thinks, *Andre has enough money to go to England for a vacation. I want to travel. I will go and see Andre. He will be very pleased to see me. He will take me to England for a vacation.*

The next day Sofia takes a taxi to Andre's house. She is wearing her best jeans. Her makeup is perfect. She knows she looks good. When the taxi stops at Andre's house, Sofia cannot believe her eyes. The house is big. The garden is beautiful. It looks like a rich man's house. Next to the house is a big car.

This is a good idea, thinks Sofia. *He has a big house and a big car. The car is old, but he will buy a new one for me.*

She tells the taxi driver to wait. She goes to the front door and knocks. Andre answers the door. He is very surprised to see Sofia.

"Andre I missed you!" says Sofia. "Please pay the taxi driver. I have no money."

Sofia walks into the house. Andre goes out and pays the taxi driver. He uses all his money.

He goes back into the house. Sofia is walking around the house looking at everything. She looks at the bathroom. "It is very old-fashioned," she says.

"I like it," says Andre. "I wanted an old-style bathroom. Come into the living room. I will make you some coffee."

Andre takes Sofia into the living room. She sits down. Andre goes to the kitchen to make coffee. *Why is she here?* he wonders. *I don't want her in my house.*

Sofia sits in the living room. She looks at the furniture.

It's very old, she thinks. *I will tell Andre to buy new modern furniture. The curtains are ugly too. I will choose some nice new curtains. The room is big. I can ask my friends to come here for parties.*

Andre comes into the room with coffee.

"Oh Andre. I'm so happy to see you. You have been so busy. Too busy for me. I have been so lonely!" says Sofia. "But you have been busy with this house. You can make this a nice house. I will help you."

"I called you many times," says Andre. "You wouldn't talk to me."

"Oh, that was nothing," answers Sofia. "You should call me every day until I talk to you."

"You had another boyfriend."

"I was lonely. But I love you."

Andre is not happy to see Sofia. "Why did you come here?" he asks.

Sofia stands up and holds Andre's hands. "I love you. Petr told me you are going to England. I don't want you to go to England without me. I'll come with you and look after you. We'll have a wonderful time."

Andre pulls his hands away. "I only have enough money for a ticket for one person."

"Oh," answers Sofia. "Well let's go somewhere else. You can sell your ticket for England and we'll go to Italy. There will be enough money for two people to go to Italy. I've always wanted to go to Italy."

"Sofia." Andre wants to laugh. "I am going to England. I am going alone. I will take you back to the city now. I am busy and I have to meet someone."

"I'll come with you," says Sofia.

"You will not." Andre is angry now. "I am going now. You can come with me and I will drive you home. Or you can walk."

Andre picks up his keys and walks to the door. He holds the door open for Sofia. Sofia goes out and gets into the car.

She is quiet for a few minutes while Andre drives into the city. Then she says, "I want a car. You won't use your car while you are in England. Can I use your car?"

"No," says Andre.

Sofia talks and talks. Andre doesn't listen. He thinks, *I was crazy. I thought I was in love with her. But she is not a nice person. She is not very clever either.*

Finally, they arrive outside Sofia's parents' house.

Sofia gets out of the car. "Bring me back a nice present from England," she says.

Andre drives away. He thinks about his life last year and his life now. Last year he was very much in love with Sofia. He had no money. He lived in a small apartment. He only had one dream. His dream was to marry Sofia.

Now he has more friends, a car and a beautiful house. He has learned to speak English. He has a new job and he is going to England!

I will buy Sofia a present, he thinks. *A very small one. But I will buy her something. All these good things happened to me because Sofia wanted me to buy a house. So, I should buy her a small 'thank you' present!*

THANK YOU

Thank you for reading Andre's Dream! We hope you enjoyed Andre's story. (Word count: 7,620)

There are quizzes about this book on our free study site I Talk You Talk Press EXTRA. http://italk-youtalk.com

If you would like to read more graded readers, please visit our website
http://www.italkyoutalk.com

Other Level 2 graded readers include
Adventure in Rome
A Passion for Music
Christmas Tales
Danger in Seattle
Don't Come Back
Finders Keepers…
Marcy's Bakery
Men's Konkatsu Tales
Salaryman Secrets!
Stories for Halloween
The Perfect Wedding
The House in the Forest

ABOUT THE AUTHOR

I Talk You Talk Press is a Japan-based publisher of language textbooks, graded readers and language learning/teaching resources.

Our team is made up of highly experienced language teachers and translators, who have all studied at least one additional language to an advanced level.

This experience enables us to design our materials from the perspective of both the teacher and the learner. We consult with both teachers and language learners when designing our textbooks and graded readers, and test our materials extensively in the classroom before publication.

We are a fast-growing press, and currently publish graded readers for learners of English. We publish new graded readers monthly.